HOW TO
CONQUER
YOUR
FEAR OF FAILURE

"Mastering Fear: Overcoming the
Roadblocks to Success"

VINCENT HOWELL

Table of Contents

Dedication

To all who have ever felt the suffocating grip of fear, this book is dedicated to you. In the pursuit of dreams and aspirations, fear often stands as an imposing barrier, threatening to derail our progress and stifle our potential. Yet, it is in confronting this fear that true growth and empowerment emerge. This dedication is a testament to your courage, resilience, and unwavering determination to conquer the formidable obstacle of failure.

May these pages serve as a guiding light, illuminating the path toward overcoming self-doubt and embracing the journey of personal transformation. With each turn of the page, may you find inspiration, wisdom, and practical strategies to navigate the twists and turns of your own fear-filled terrain. Together, let us embark on a journey of discovery, as we unlock the power within to rise above adversity and emerge victorious in the face of fear.

For every individual who dares to defy the odds, shatter limitations, and rewrite their story, this dedication honors your unwavering commitment to greatness. As you embark on the quest to conquer your fear of failure, remember that you are not alone. Within these words lies a reservoir of hope, encouragement, and support, guiding you toward a future defined not by fear, but by boundless possibility. Here's to embracing the challenge, seizing the moment, and triumphing over fear, one courageous step at a time.

Acknowledgments

who have contributed to the realization of this book. To my family, whose unwavering love and support have been the bedrock of my journey, thank you for standing by me through every triumph and tribulation. Your belief in me has been a constant source of strength and inspiration.

To my mentors and colleagues, whose wisdom and guidance have illuminated my path, I am profoundly grateful for your invaluable insights and encouragement. Your expertise has enriched the pages of this book and empowered me to navigate the complexities of conquering fear with clarity and purpose.

Finally, to the readers who have entrusted me with their time and attention, thank you for embarking on this transformative journey with me. It is my sincerest hope that the lessons shared within these pages will empower you to confront your fears with courage and resilience, paving the way for a future defined by boundless possibility and unparalleled success.

Introduction

In the pursuit of our dreams and aspirations, one formidable adversary often looms large: the fear of failure. It's a pervasive force, capable of paralyzing even the most determined souls, rendering them hesitant to take the bold steps necessary for success. Yet, it is precisely in confronting this fear that we unlock the door to our greatest potential. Welcome to "Conquer Your Fear of Failure," a guidebook designed to illuminate the path toward overcoming the insidious grip of self-doubt and embracing the journey of personal transformation.

Within these pages, you'll discover practical strategies, insightful anecdotes, and empowering exercises crafted to help you navigate the tumultuous terrain of fear. Together, we'll explore the psychological underpinnings of fear, uncover the hidden blessings of failure, and harness the power of resilience to propel you toward your goals. Whether you're a budding entrepreneur, a seasoned professional, or simply someone seeking to break free from the shackles of fear, this book is your roadmap to success.

As we embark on this journey together, I invite you to cast aside the limitations of doubt and embrace the boundless possibilities that await. Let us embark on a quest to conquer fear, defy expectations, and rewrite the narrative of our lives. The time for transformation is now—let's seize it together.

Chapter 1.

Understanding Fear of Failure

- Introduction to the concept of fear of failure

Fear of failure is a deeply ingrained psychological phenomenon that can significantly impact individuals' thoughts, emotions, and behaviors. At its core, it encompasses the fear or apprehension of not meeting expectations, making mistakes, or falling short of desired goals. This fear often arises from a variety of sources, including societal pressures, personal standards, and past experiences. Individuals may develop a fear of failure due to the perceived consequences of not achieving success, such as embarrassment, disappointment, or negative judgment from others.

Furthermore, fear of failure can be fueled by perfectionism, where individuals set excessively high standards for themselves and fear any deviation from these standards. This perfectionistic mindset can lead to constant self-doubt, reluctance to take risks, and avoidance of challenges or opportunities where failure is a possibility. Additionally, the fear of failure can be exacerbated by comparison to others, as individuals may feel inadequate or inferior when they perceive others as more successful or accomplished.

Understanding the concept of fear of failure is crucial for addressing its impact on individuals' lives and well-being. By recognizing the underlying causes and manifestations of this fear, individuals can begin to develop coping strategies, such as reframing failure as a learning opportunity, setting realistic goals, and cultivating self-compassion. Moreover, fostering a supportive and understanding environment that values effort and resilience over perfection can help mitigate the negative effects of fear of failure and promote personal growth and fulfillment.

- Exploring the origins and psychology behind fear of failure

The origins of fear of failure can be traced to various psychological factors that shape individuals' beliefs, attitudes, and behaviors. One significant contributing factor is early childhood experiences, where individuals may have received praise or criticism based on their achievements or failures. Children who consistently receive validation for their successes may develop a fear of failure as they internalize the belief that their worth is contingent upon their performance.

Additionally, societal influences play a crucial role in shaping fear of failure. In cultures that prioritize achievement and success, individuals may feel immense pressure to meet high standards and avoid any form of failure. This pressure can stem from family expectations, peer comparisons, and cultural norms that equate failure with inadequacy or shame.

Moreover, cognitive processes such as cognitive distortions and irrational beliefs can perpetuate fear of failure. For example, individuals prone to catastrophizing may magnify the potential consequences of failure, leading to heightened anxiety and avoidance behaviors. Similarly, those with rigid thinking patterns may perceive failure as evidence of their inherent incompetence or unworthiness, reinforcing their fear.

From a psychological perspective, fear of failure is closely linked to self-esteem and self-efficacy. Individuals with low self-esteem may be particularly vulnerable to fear of failure, as they may interpret setbacks as confirmation of their negative self-perceptions.

Likewise, individuals with low self-efficacy, or belief in their ability to achieve goals, may avoid challenging tasks out of fear of failure, further perpetuating a cycle of avoidance and diminished confidence.

Understanding these origins and psychological mechanisms behind fear of failure is essential for effective intervention and support. By addressing underlying beliefs, challenging cognitive distortions, and fostering a growth mindset, individuals can gradually overcome their fear of failure and develop resilience in the face of challenges. Therapy, coaching, and self-help strategies aimed at building self-esteem, reframing failure as a learning opportunity, and setting realistic goals can empower individuals to pursue their aspirations with confidence and perseverance.

- Common symptoms and manifestations of fear of failure

Fear of failure can manifest in various symptoms and behaviors that can significantly impact an individual's well-being and success. Some common symptoms and manifestations include:

1. Procrastination: Individuals may procrastinate or avoid taking action on tasks or goals due to fear of not meeting expectations or making mistakes. This avoidance behavior serves as a

coping mechanism to temporarily alleviate anxiety but can ultimately hinder progress and achievement.

2. Perfectionism: Fear of failure often coexists with perfectionistic tendencies, where individuals set unrealistically high standards for themselves and fear any deviation from these standards. This perfectionistic mindset can lead to chronic dissatisfaction, self-criticism, and a reluctance to take risks.

3. Self-doubt: Individuals with fear of failure may experience pervasive self-doubt about their abilities and competence. They

may constantly second-guess themselves, downplay their achievements, and focus on their perceived shortcomings, leading to diminished self-confidence and motivation.

4. Avoidance of challenges: Fear of failure can lead individuals to avoid challenging tasks or opportunities where failure is a possibility. They may opt for safer, less demanding options to minimize the risk of disappointment or embarrassment, ultimately limiting their personal and professional growth.

5. Negative self-talk: Internal dialogue characterized by self-criticism, pessimism, and catastrophic thinking is common among individuals with fear of failure. They may engage in negative self-talk, such as "I'm not good enough" or "I'll never succeed," which reinforces their fears and undermines their self-esteem.

6. Physical symptoms: Fear of failure can also manifest in physical symptoms such as tension, muscle tightness, sweating, trembling, or gastrointestinal distress. These physiological reactions are the

body's natural response to stress and anxiety triggered by the anticipation of failure.

7. Social withdrawal: Individuals with fear of failure may withdraw from social interactions or avoid situations where they might be evaluated or judged by others. They may fear being exposed as incompetent or inadequate, leading to social isolation and feelings of loneliness.

Recognizing these symptoms and manifestations is crucial for addressing fear of failure and promoting resilience and growth. Seeking support from friends, family, or mental health professionals can provide valuable guidance and encouragement in overcoming fear and pursuing personal and professional goals with confidence.

Chapter 2.

Identifying Your Fear Triggers

- Self-assessment exercises to pinpoint specific triggers

Identifying your fear triggers is essential for understanding and addressing your fear of failure. Here are some self-assessment exercises to help pinpoint specific triggers:

1. Reflection on past experiences: Take some time to reflect on past

experiences where you felt fearful or anxious about failure. What were the circumstances surrounding those experiences? Were there specific situations, tasks, or goals that triggered your fear? Identifying recurring patterns can help you pinpoint common triggers.

2. Journaling: Keep a journal to track your thoughts, emotions, and behaviors related to fear of failure. Write down any situations or events that evoke fear, as well as the thoughts and feelings you experience in those moments. This can help you identify patterns

and underlying beliefs contributing to your fear.

3. Mindfulness exercises: Practice mindfulness techniques, such as deep breathing, meditation, or body scans, to become more aware of your thoughts and emotions in the present moment. Pay attention to any signs of anxiety or fear that arise and explore the underlying triggers.

4. Self-assessment questionnaires: Use self-assessment questionnaires or quizzes designed to identify fear of failure and related triggers. These tools can provide insights

into your fears, beliefs, and coping strategies, helping you pinpoint specific areas to focus on.

5. Seek feedback from others: Ask trusted friends, family members, or mentors for feedback on your behavior and tendencies related to fear of failure. They may offer valuable insights and observations that you may not have noticed on your own.

By engaging in these self-assessment exercises, you can gain a better understanding of your fear triggers and develop strategies to manage and overcome them. Remember that identifying your triggers is the first step towards building resilience and pursuing your goals with confidence.

- Recognizing patterns and situations that exacerbate fear of failure

Recognizing patterns and situations that exacerbate fear of failure is crucial for effectively managing and overcoming this fear. Here are some steps to help identify these patterns:

1. Reflect on past experiences: Take time to reflect on past situations where you felt intense fear of failure. Consider the circumstances, triggers, and your emotional and behavioral responses. Look for commonalities and recurring themes that may indicate specific patterns.

2. Track your emotions: Keep a journal or use a mood tracking app to record your emotions throughout the day. Pay attention to moments when you experience heightened anxiety, self-doubt, or avoidance behaviors. Note the

context and triggers associated with these emotions.

3. Identify avoidance behaviors: Notice any patterns of avoidance or procrastination in your behavior. Are there certain tasks or situations that you consistently avoid due to fear of failure? Identifying these avoidance behaviors can help pinpoint specific triggers.

4. Analyze cognitive distortions: Examine your thought patterns and cognitive distortions that contribute to fear of failure. Common distortions include catastrophizing (assuming the

worst possible outcome), black-and-white thinking (seeing situations as all good or all bad), and personalization (blaming oneself for external events). Recognizing these distortions can help challenge and reframe negative thinking patterns.

5. Consider situational factors: Evaluate the impact of specific situations or environments on your fear of failure. For example, you may notice that you feel more anxious when working under tight deadlines or when receiving feedback from authority figures. Understanding how different situations influence your fear can

help you develop coping strategies.

6. Seek feedback: Ask for feedback from trusted friends, family members, or colleagues about your behavior and reactions in stressful situations. They may provide valuable insights and observations that can help you identify patterns that you may not have noticed on your own.

By recognizing patterns and situations that exacerbate fear of failure, you can gain a deeper understanding of your triggers and develop effective strategies to manage and overcome this fear.

Remember that self-awareness is the first step towards building resilience and achieving personal and professional growth.

- Understanding how past experiences contribute to present fears

Understanding how past experiences contribute to present fears is essential for addressing and overcoming fear of failure. Here are some key points to consider:

1. Early Childhood Experiences: Reflect on your upbringing and early experiences with success and failure. Consider how your caregivers, teachers, or peers responded to your achievements and mistakes. Positive reinforcement for success and criticism or punishment for failure can shape your beliefs and attitudes towards success and failure later in life.

2. Traumatic Events: Traumatic experiences, such as significant failures or humiliating situations, can leave lasting emotional scars and contribute to fear of failure.

These events may create deep-seated beliefs about one's incompetence or unworthiness, leading to heightened anxiety and avoidance behaviors in similar situations.

3. Cultural and Societal Influences: Cultural and societal norms surrounding success and failure can significantly impact individuals' perceptions and fears. In cultures that emphasize achievement and perfectionism, individuals may internalize high standards and fear the consequences of falling short. Additionally, societal pressures to meet certain expectations or

conform to specific standards can exacerbate fear of failure.

4. Past Rejections or Criticisms: Rejections, criticisms, or negative feedback from authority figures, peers, or romantic partners can contribute to feelings of inadequacy and fear of failure. These experiences may lead individuals to doubt their abilities, fear judgment from others, and avoid situations where they might face rejection or criticism again.

5. Learned Behavior: Observing how others, such as parents, siblings, or role models, respond to failure can also influence one's

fear of failure. If individuals witness others reacting with fear, avoidance, or harsh self-criticism to failure, they may internalize similar behaviors and beliefs.

6. Cumulative Effect: It's important to recognize that fear of failure often develops gradually over time through a combination of various past experiences. Each experience, whether positive or negative, contributes to shaping one's beliefs, attitudes, and coping mechanisms related to failure.

By understanding how past experiences contribute to present

fears, individuals can begin to challenge and reframe their beliefs, develop self-compassion, and cultivate resilience in the face of failure. Therapy, self-reflection, and support from others can be valuable tools in this process of healing and personal growth.

Chapter 3.

Challenging Negative Beliefs

- Strategies for identifying and reframing negative beliefs

Challenging negative beliefs is essential for overcoming fear of failure and fostering resilience. Here are some strategies for identifying and reframing negative beliefs:

1. Awareness: Start by becoming aware of your negative beliefs

about failure. Notice the thoughts and self-talk that arise when you face challenges or setbacks. Write down these beliefs and pay attention to any patterns or recurring themes.

2. Questioning: Challenge your negative beliefs by questioning their accuracy and validity. Ask yourself:
    - Is there evidence to support this belief?
        - Are there alternative interpretations or explanations for the situation?
    - Would I say the same thing to a friend in a similar situation?

3. Reality Testing: Test the validity of your negative beliefs by examining past experiences. Look for instances where your beliefs were disproven or where failure led to growth and learning rather than catastrophe. Use these examples to challenge the absoluteness of your negative beliefs.

4. Cognitive Restructuring: Replace negative beliefs with more balanced and realistic thoughts. Reframe failures as opportunities for growth and learning rather than indicators of incompetence or worthlessness. Practice affirmations and positive

self-talk to reinforce these new beliefs.

5. Behavioral Experiments: Conduct behavioral experiments to test the validity of your negative beliefs in real-life situations. Take small steps outside your comfort zone and observe the outcomes. Use these experiences to gather evidence that contradicts your negative beliefs and reinforces more positive ones.

6. Seeking Perspective: Seek feedback and perspective from others to challenge your negative beliefs. Talk to friends, family members, or mentors about your

fears and listen to their insights and reassurances. Often, others can offer a more balanced and objective view of your abilities and potential.

7. Mindfulness and Acceptance: Practice mindfulness and acceptance techniques to cultivate self-compassion and non-judgmental awareness of your thoughts and feelings. Recognize that negative beliefs are a natural part of being human and that you have the power to choose how you respond to them.

By implementing these strategies, you can gradually challenge and reframe your negative beliefs about failure, leading to increased resilience, self-confidence, and a healthier relationship with success and setbacks. Remember that change takes time and effort, so be patient and compassionate with yourself throughout this process.

- Cognitive behavioral techniques to overcome irrational thoughts

Cognitive-behavioral techniques (CBT) are highly effective for overcoming irrational thoughts, including those related to fear of failure. Here are some CBT techniques specifically tailored to address irrational thoughts:

1. Identify and Challenge Negative Thoughts: Start by identifying irrational thoughts related to failure, such as "I must succeed at everything I do" or "Failure is unacceptable." Challenge these thoughts by examining the evidence for and against them. Ask yourself if there is any proof that supports these thoughts and

if there are more balanced and realistic perspectives to consider.

2. Cognitive Restructuring: Replace irrational thoughts with more rational and balanced alternatives. For example, instead of thinking, "If I fail, it means I'm incompetent," reframe it as, "Failure is a natural part of learning and growth, and it doesn't define my worth as a person."

3. Thought Records: Keep a thought diary to track your irrational thoughts, the situations that trigger them, and your emotional responses. Use thought records to analyze and challenge

these thoughts systematically, noting any distortions or cognitive errors.

4. Evidence Gathering: Gather evidence to support or refute your irrational thoughts. Look for examples from your own life, as well as from others, where failure has led to positive outcomes or growth. Use this evidence to challenge the absoluteness of your negative beliefs.

5. Behavioral Experiments: Conduct behavioral experiments to test the validity of your irrational thoughts. Purposefully engage in activities that trigger fear of failure

and observe the outcomes. Use these experiments to gather evidence that contradicts your irrational beliefs and reinforces more adaptive thinking patterns.

6. Mindfulness and Acceptance: Practice mindfulness techniques to cultivate awareness of your irrational thoughts without judgment or attachment. Accept that these thoughts are normal and natural, but also recognize that they do not necessarily reflect reality. Mindfulness can help you develop a sense of detachment from your thoughts and reduce their power over you.

7. Graded Exposure: Gradually expose yourself to situations that trigger fear of failure, starting with less challenging scenarios and progressively increasing the difficulty. This gradual exposure allows you to build confidence and resilience in handling failure-related stressors.

By incorporating these cognitive-behavioral techniques into your daily routine, you can effectively challenge and overcome irrational thoughts related to fear of failure. However, if you find it challenging to implement these techniques on your own, consider seeking support from a qualified therapist who can provide personalized guidance and assistance.

- Cultivating a growth mindset to embrace challenges and setbacks

Cultivating a growth mindset is essential for embracing challenges and setbacks, and it can significantly help in overcoming fear of failure. Here are some strategies to develop and foster a growth mindset:

1.   View   Challenges   as Opportunities: Instead of seeing challenges as threats to your abilities or worth, view them as opportunities for growth and learning. Embrace challenges with a positive attitude, knowing that they can help you develop new skills, resilience, and character.

2.   Focus   on   Effort   and Persistence: Shift your focus from outcomes to the process of growth and improvement. Value effort and persistence over innate talent or intelligence.   Recognize   that success often requires hard work, perseverance, and resilience in the face of obstacles.

3. Learn from Setbacks: Embrace setbacks as valuable learning experiences rather than signs of failure or inadequacy. Reflect on what went wrong, identify lessons learned, and use this knowledge to adapt and improve your approach in the future.

4. Challenge Fixed Beliefs: Challenge and reframe fixed beliefs about intelligence, talent, and success. Instead of believing that abilities are fixed and unchangeable, recognize that skills can be developed and improved over time with practice, effort, and effective strategies.

5. Encourage Self-Compassion: Practice self-compassion and kindness towards yourself, especially when facing challenges or setbacks. Treat yourself with the same understanding and support that you would offer to a friend in a similar situation. Acknowledge your efforts and progress, regardless of the outcome.

6. Celebrate Growth and Progress: Celebrate your growth and progress, no matter how small. Recognize and acknowledge your achievements, milestones, and improvements

along the way. This positive reinforcement can reinforce your belief in your ability to grow and succeed.

7. Seek Feedback and Support: Be open to feedback from others and use it as an opportunity for growth and development. Surround yourself with supportive individuals who encourage and challenge you to reach your full potential.

By cultivating a growth mindset, you can approach challenges and setbacks with resilience, optimism, and a willingness to learn and grow. Over time, this mindset shift can help you overcome fear of failure and achieve greater success and fulfillment in your personal and professional endeavors.

Chapter 4.

Building Resilience and Confidence

- Developing resilience through adversity

Building resilience and confidence is crucial for navigating life's challenges and achieving personal growth. One key aspect of this process is developing resilience through adversity. When faced with difficulties, individuals have the opportunity to build resilience by learning to adapt and persevere. Each setback becomes a chance to strengthen one's ability to bounce back and overcome obstacles. By reframing challenges as opportunities for growth, individuals can cultivate a mindset that fosters resilience.

Moreover, facing adversity can help individuals discover their inner strength and capabilities. Overcoming obstacles, whether they are personal, professional, or academic, allows individuals to recognize their capacity to endure and thrive in the face of hardship. This self-awareness contributes to the development of confidence, as individuals gain a deeper understanding of their resilience and ability to overcome adversity.

Building resilience and confidence also involves developing coping strategies to manage stress and uncertainty effectively. Learning to regulate emotions, maintain a positive outlook, and seek support when needed are essential skills for navigating life's ups and downs. By honing these coping mechanisms, individuals can cultivate a sense of control and mastery over challenging situations, further boosting their confidence and resilience.

Ultimately, building resilience and confidence is an ongoing process that requires practice and self-reflection. By embracing adversity as an opportunity for growth, recognizing one's inner strength, and developing effective coping strategies, individuals can enhance their resilience and confidence, empowering them to thrive in the face of life's uncertainties.

- Practical techniques for boosting self-confidence

Boosting self-confidence involves adopting practical techniques that focus on self-improvement and positive self-perception. One effective technique is setting achievable goals and celebrating small victories. Breaking down larger goals into manageable steps allows individuals to track progress and build confidence as they accomplish each step.

Additionally, practicing self-care and maintaining a healthy lifestyle can significantly impact self-confidence. Engaging in regular exercise, eating nutritious foods, and prioritizing adequate sleep contribute to overall well-being, which in turn fosters a positive self-image and confidence.

Another practical technique is to challenge negative self-talk and replace it with affirming statements. Recognizing and reframing negative thoughts allows individuals to cultivate a more optimistic and empowering mindset, boosting self-confidence in the process.

Moreover, stepping out of comfort zones and embracing new experiences can help individuals expand their capabilities and build confidence. Whether it's trying a new hobby, taking on a leadership role, or speaking up in a group setting, pushing past fear and discomfort fosters personal growth and confidence.

Lastly, seeking feedback and constructive criticism from trusted individuals can provide valuable insights and validation, reinforcing one's strengths and abilities. Accepting feedback gracefully and using it as an opportunity for growth can bolster self-confidence over time.

By incorporating these practical techniques into daily routines, individuals can gradually build self-confidence and develop a strong sense of self-assurance to navigate life's challenges with resilience and optimism.

- Setting realistic goals and celebrating progress

Setting realistic goals and celebrating progress is a powerful technique for boosting self-confidence. When setting goals, it's important to make them specific, measurable, achievable, relevant, and time-bound (SMART). Setting realistic goals ensures that they are attainable, which sets individuals up for success and boosts confidence as they make progress.

Breaking down larger goals into smaller, manageable tasks makes them less overwhelming and allows for incremental progress. Each step achieved serves as a milestone to celebrate, reinforcing a sense of accomplishment and boosting self-confidence. Celebrating progress can take various forms, such as acknowledging achievements, rewarding oneself, or sharing successes with others.

Moreover, reflecting on progress allows individuals to recognize their efforts and the obstacles they've overcome along the way. This reflection fosters a positive self-perception and reinforces the belief in one's abilities, further enhancing self-confidence.

Additionally, keeping track of progress through journaling, using apps, or visual aids like progress charts can provide a tangible reminder of achievements, serving as motivation to continue striving towards goals.

It's essential to celebrate not only major milestones but also small victories and progress made towards long-term goals. Each step forward, no matter how small, contributes to overall progress and deserves recognition.

By setting realistic goals and celebrating progress, individuals build momentum, cultivate a positive mindset, and ultimately boost their self-confidence, empowering them to tackle new challenges with resilience and optimism.

Chapter 5.

Taking Action and Moving Forward

- Step-by-step action plans for confronting fear of failure

Confronting the fear of failure requires deliberate action and a step-by-step approach to gradually overcome apprehensions. Firstly, acknowledge and accept the fear, understanding that it's a natural response to the unknown. Then, break down the fear-inducing task or goal into smaller, manageable steps. This approach makes the process less daunting and allows for a sense of accomplishment with each completed step.

Next, challenge negative thoughts associated with failure by reframing them into more realistic and empowering perspectives. Practice self-compassion and remind yourself that failure is not a reflection of your worth as a person but rather an opportunity for growth and learning.

Developing a support system of friends, family, or mentors who can provide encouragement and guidance can be immensely helpful. Share your fears and goals with them, and lean on their support when facing challenges.

Set specific deadlines for each step of the action plan to maintain momentum and accountability. Breaking the process into manageable timelines ensures steady progress and prevents procrastination.

Visualize success and focus on the potential rewards of overcoming the fear of failure. Visualizing positive outcomes can motivate action and build confidence in your ability to confront challenges head-on.

Lastly, take the first step, even if it's small, and gradually increase the level of difficulty as you build confidence. Celebrate each success along the way, no matter how minor, and use them as fuel to propel you forward.

By following a step-by-step action plan, confronting the fear of failure becomes more manageable, allowing individuals to move forward with courage and resilience towards their goals.

- Implementing strategies to push through discomfort and uncertainty

Implementing strategies to push through discomfort and uncertainty is essential for personal growth and achieving goals. One effective strategy is to practice mindfulness and stay present in the moment. By focusing on the present instead of worrying about the future or dwelling on past failures, individuals can reduce feelings of discomfort and uncertainty, allowing them to take action with greater clarity and confidence.

Another strategy is to reframe negative thoughts and self-doubt into more positive and empowering beliefs. Recognize that discomfort and uncertainty are natural parts of the growth process, and view them as opportunities for learning and development rather than obstacles to be avoided.

Setting realistic expectations and acknowledging that progress may be gradual can help individuals navigate discomfort and uncertainty more effectively. Break down tasks into smaller, manageable steps, and celebrate each small victory along the way to maintain motivation and momentum.

Seeking support from friends, family, or mentors can provide encouragement and guidance during times of uncertainty. Surrounding oneself with a supportive network of individuals who believe in their abilities can bolster confidence and help individuals push through discomfort.

Additionally, embracing vulnerability and being open to taking risks can lead to personal growth and new opportunities.

Stepping outside of comfort zones and embracing uncertainty allows individuals to expand their capabilities and develop resilience in the face of adversity.

Ultimately, pushing through discomfort and uncertainty requires courage, perseverance, and a willingness to embrace the unknown. By implementing these strategies and adopting a positive mindset, individuals can navigate challenges with greater ease and confidence, ultimately achieving their goals and realizing their full potential.

- Maintaining momentum and staying motivated on the path to success

Maintaining momentum and staying motivated on the path to success requires consistency, perseverance, and a proactive approach. One effective strategy is to break down long-term goals into smaller, manageable tasks. By focusing on these smaller tasks, individuals can maintain a sense of progress and momentum, which helps to sustain motivation over time.

Setting clear and achievable milestones along the way provides a roadmap for success and allows individuals to track their progress. Celebrating each milestone reached, no matter how small, reinforces a sense of accomplishment and keeps motivation levels high.

Additionally, maintaining a positive mindset and staying optimistic, even in the face of setbacks, is crucial for staying motivated. Viewing challenges as opportunities for growth rather than insurmountable obstacles helps individuals stay resilient and focused on their goals.

Finding inspiration from role models or mentors who have achieved similar goals can also help individuals stay motivated. Learning from their experiences and seeking guidance when needed can provide encouragement and renewed determination to continue moving forward.

Moreover, incorporating self-care practices into daily routines, such as exercise, meditation, and adequate rest, helps individuals recharge both physically and mentally, enabling them to stay motivated and focused on their goals.

Lastly, staying connected with a supportive network of friends, family, or peers who share similar aspirations can provide encouragement, accountability, and motivation along the journey.

By implementing these strategies and staying committed to their goals, individuals can maintain momentum and stay motivated on the path to success, ultimately achieving their desired outcomes and realizing their full potential.

www.ingramcontent.com/pod-product-compliance
Lightning Source LLC
Chambersburg PA
CBHW051835250726
48659CB00005B/1846